This
WEEKLY MEAL
planner

Belongs To:

_____

WEEKLY MEAL
planner

	BREAKFAST	LUNCH	DINNER
Monday			
Tuesday			
Wednesday			
Thursday			
Friday			
Saturday			
Sunday			

WEEK _____

GROCERY *list*

MEAT & SEAFOOD	FRUIT & VEGETABLES	DAIRY

FROZEN GOODS	PANTRY ITEMS	BAKERY & DELI

NOTES:

WEEKLY MEAL
planner

	BREAKFAST	LUNCH	DINNER
Monday			
Tuesday			
Wednesday			
Thursday			
Friday			
Saturday			
Sunday			

WEEK _____

GROCERY *list*

MEAT & SEAFOOD

FRUIT & VEGETABLES

DAIRY

FROZEN GOODS

PANTRY ITEMS

BAKERY & DELI

NOTES:

WEEKLY MEAL
planner

	BREAKFAST	LUNCH	DINNER
Monday			
Tuesday			
Wednesday			
Thursday			
Friday			
Saturday			
Sunday			

WEEK _____

GROCERY *list*

MEAT & SEAFOOD

....
....
....
....
....
....
....
....

FRUIT & VEGETABLES

....
....
....
....
....
....
....
....

DAIRY

....
....
....
....
....
....
....
....

FROZEN GOODS

....
....
....
....
....
....
....
....

PANTRY ITEMS

....
....
....
....
....
....
....
....

BAKERY & DELI

....
....
....
....
....
....
....
....

NOTES:

WEEKLY MEAL
planner

	BREAKFAST	LUNCH	DINNER
Monday			
Tuesday			
Wednesday			
Thursday			
Friday			
Saturday			
Sunday			

WEEK _____

GROCERY *list*

MEAT & SEAFOOD	FRUIT & VEGETABLES	DAIRY

FROZEN GOODS	PANTRY ITEMS	BAKERY & DELI

NOTES:

WEEKLY MEAL
planner

	BREAKFAST	LUNCH	DINNER
Monday			
Tuesday			
Wednesday			
Thursday			
Friday			
Saturday			
Sunday			

WEEK _____

GROCERY *list*

MEAT & SEAFOOD

FRUIT & VEGETABLES

DAIRY

FROZEN GOODS

PANTRY ITEMS

BAKERY & DELI

NOTES:

WEEKLY MEAL
planner

	BREAKFAST	LUNCH	DINNER
Monday			
Tuesday			
Wednesday			
Thursday			
Friday			
Saturday			
Sunday			

WEEK _____

GROCERY *list*

MEAT & SEAFOOD	FRUIT & VEGETABLES	DAIRY

FROZEN GOODS	PANTRY ITEMS	BAKERY & DELI

NOTES:

WEEKLY MEAL
planner

	BREAKFAST	LUNCH	DINNER
Monday			
Tuesday			
Wednesday			
Thursday			
Friday			
Saturday			
Sunday			

WEEK _____

GROCERY *list*

MEAT & SEAFOOD

....
....
....
....
....
....
....
....

FRUIT & VEGETABLES

....
....
....
....
....
....
....
....

DAIRY

....
....
....
....
....
....
....
....

FROZEN GOODS

....
....
....
....
....
....
....
....

PANTRY ITEMS

....
....
....
....
....
....
....
....

BAKERY & DELI

....
....
....
....
....
....
....
....

NOTES:

WEEKLY MEAL
planner

	BREAKFAST	LUNCH	DINNER
Monday			
Tuesday			
Wednesday			
Thursday			
Friday			
Saturday			
Sunday			

WEEK _____

GROCERY *list*

MEAT & SEAFOOD	FRUIT & VEGETABLES	DAIRY

FROZEN GOODS	PANTRY ITEMS	BAKERY & DELI

NOTES:

WEEKLY MEAL
planner

	BREAKFAST	LUNCH	DINNER
Monday			
Tuesday			
Wednesday			
Thursday			
Friday			
Saturday			
Sunday			

WEEK _____

GROCERY *list*

MEAT & SEAFOOD	FRUIT & VEGETABLES	DAIRY

FROZEN GOODS	PANTRY ITEMS	BAKERY & DELI

NOTES:

WEEKLY MEAL
planner

	BREAKFAST	LUNCH	DINNER
Monday			
Tuesday			
Wednesday			
Thursday			
Friday			
Saturday			
Sunday			

WEEK _____

GROCERY *list*

MEAT & SEAFOOD

FRUIT & VEGETABLES

DAIRY

FROZEN GOODS

PANTRY ITEMS

BAKERY & DELI

NOTES:

WEEKLY MEAL
planner

	BREAKFAST	LUNCH	DINNER
Monday			
Tuesday			
Wednesday			
Thursday			
Friday			
Saturday			
Sunday			

WEEK _____

GROCERY *list*

MEAT & SEAFOOD

FRUIT & VEGETABLES

DAIRY

FROZEN GOODS

PANTRY ITEMS

BAKERY & DELI

NOTES:

WEEKLY MEAL
planner

	BREAKFAST	LUNCH	DINNER
Monday			
Tuesday			
Wednesday			
Thursday			
Friday			
Saturday			
Sunday			

WEEK _____

GROCERY *list*

MEAT & SEAFOOD

....
....
....
....
....
....
....
....

FRUIT & VEGETABLES

....
....
....
....
....
....
....
....

DAIRY

....
....
....
....
....
....
....
....

FROZEN GOODS

....
....
....
....
....
....
....
....

PANTRY ITEMS

....
....
....
....
....
....
....
....

BAKERY & DELI

....
....
....
....
....
....
....
....

NOTES:

WEEKLY MEAL
planner

	BREAKFAST	LUNCH	DINNER
Monday			
Tuesday			
Wednesday			
Thursday			
Friday			
Saturday			
Sunday			

WEEK _____

GROCERY *list*

MEAT & SEAFOOD

....
....
....
....
....
....
....
....
....
....

FRUIT & VEGETABLES

....
....
....
....
....
....
....
....
....
....

DAIRY

....
....
....
....
....
....
....
....
....
....

FROZEN GOODS

....
....
....
....
....
....
....
....
....

PANTRY ITEMS

....
....
....
....
....
....
....
....
....

BAKERY & DELI

....
....
....
....
....
....
....
....
....

NOTES:

WEEKLY MEAL
planner

	BREAKFAST	LUNCH	DINNER
Monday			
Tuesday			
Wednesday			
Thursday			
Friday			
Saturday			
Sunday			

WEEK _____

GROCERY *list*

MEAT & SEAFOOD	FRUIT & VEGETABLES	DAIRY

FROZEN GOODS	PANTRY ITEMS	BAKERY & DELI

NOTES:

WEEKLY MEAL
planner

	BREAKFAST	LUNCH	DINNER
Monday			
Tuesday			
Wednesday			
Thursday			
Friday			
Saturday			
Sunday			

WEEK _____

GROCERY *list*

MEAT & SEAFOOD

....
....
....
....
....
....
....
....

FRUIT & VEGETABLES

....
....
....
....
....
....
....
....

DAIRY

....
....
....
....
....
....
....
....

FROZEN GOODS

....
....
....
....
....
....
....
....

PANTRY ITEMS

....
....
....
....
....
....
....
....

BAKERY & DELI

....
....
....
....
....
....
....
....

NOTES:

WEEKLY MEAL
planner

	BREAKFAST	LUNCH	DINNER
Monday			
Tuesday			
Wednesday			
Thursday			
Friday			
Saturday			
Sunday			

WEEK _____

GROCERY *list*

MEAT & SEAFOOD	FRUIT & VEGETABLES	DAIRY

FROZEN GOODS	PANTRY ITEMS	BAKERY & DELI

NOTES:

WEEKLY MEAL
planner

	BREAKFAST	LUNCH	DINNER
Monday			
Tuesday			
Wednesday			
Thursday			
Friday			
Saturday			
Sunday			

WEEK _____

GROCERY *list*

MEAT & SEAFOOD

FRUIT & VEGETABLES

DAIRY

FROZEN GOODS

PANTRY ITEMS

BAKERY & DELI

NOTES:

WEEKLY MEAL
planner

	BREAKFAST	LUNCH	DINNER
Monday			
Tuesday			
Wednesday			
Thursday			
Friday			
Saturday			
Sunday			

WEEK _____

GROCERY *list*

MEAT & SEAFOOD	FRUIT & VEGETABLES	DAIRY

FROZEN GOODS	PANTRY ITEMS	BAKERY & DELI

NOTES:

WEEKLY MEAL
planner

	BREAKFAST	LUNCH	DINNER
Monday			
Tuesday			
Wednesday			
Thursday			
Friday			
Saturday			
Sunday			

WEEK _____

GROCERY *list*

MEAT & SEAFOOD

FRUIT & VEGETABLES

DAIRY

FROZEN GOODS

PANTRY ITEMS

BAKERY & DELI

NOTES:

WEEKLY MEAL
planner

	BREAKFAST	LUNCH	DINNER
Monday			
Tuesday			
Wednesday			
Thursday			
Friday			
Saturday			
Sunday			

WEEK _____

GROCERY *list*

MEAT & SEAFOOD

....
....
....
....
....
....
....
....

FRUIT & VEGETABLES

....
....
....
....
....
....
....
....

DAIRY

....
....
....
....
....
....
....
....

FROZEN GOODS

....
....
....
....
....
....
....
....

PANTRY ITEMS

....
....
....
....
....
....
....
....

BAKERY & DELI

....
....
....
....
....
....
....
....

NOTES:

WEEKLY MEAL
planner

	BREAKFAST	LUNCH	DINNER
Monday			
Tuesday			
Wednesday			
Thursday			
Friday			
Saturday			
Sunday			

WEEK _____

GROCERY *list*

MEAT & SEAFOOD

FRUIT & VEGETABLES

DAIRY

FROZEN GOODS

PANTRY ITEMS

BAKERY & DELI

NOTES:

WEEKLY MEAL
planner

	BREAKFAST	LUNCH	DINNER
Monday			
Tuesday			
Wednesday			
Thursday			
Friday			
Saturday			
Sunday			

WEEK _____

GROCERY *list*

MEAT & SEAFOOD

FRUIT & VEGETABLES

DAIRY

FROZEN GOODS

PANTRY ITEMS

BAKERY & DELI

NOTES:

WEEKLY MEAL
planner

	BREAKFAST	LUNCH	DINNER
Monday			
Tuesday			
Wednesday			
Thursday			
Friday			
Saturday			
Sunday			

WEEK _____

GROCERY *list*

MEAT & SEAFOOD	FRUIT & VEGETABLES	DAIRY

FROZEN GOODS	PANTRY ITEMS	BAKERY & DELI

NOTES:

WEEKLY MEAL
planner

	BREAKFAST	LUNCH	DINNER
Monday			
Tuesday			
Wednesday			
Thursday			
Friday			
Saturday			
Sunday			

WEEK _____

GROCERY *list*

MEAT & SEAFOOD	FRUIT & VEGETABLES	DAIRY

FROZEN GOODS	PANTRY ITEMS	BAKERY & DELI

NOTES:

WEEKLY MEAL
planner

	BREAKFAST	LUNCH	DINNER
Monday			
Tuesday			
Wednesday			
Thursday			
Friday			
Saturday			
Sunday			

WEEK _____

GROCERY *list*

MEAT & SEAFOOD

....
....
....
....
....
....
....
....

FRUIT & VEGETABLES

....
....
....
....
....
....
....
....

DAIRY

....
....
....
....
....
....
....
....

FROZEN GOODS

....
....
....
....
....
....
....
....

PANTRY ITEMS

....
....
....
....
....
....
....
....

BAKERY & DELI

....
....
....
....
....
....
....
....

NOTES:

WEEKLY MEAL
planner

	BREAKFAST	LUNCH	DINNER
Monday			
Tuesday			
Wednesday			
Thursday			
Friday			
Saturday			
Sunday			

WEEK _____

GROCERY *list*

MEAT & SEAFOOD

FRUIT & VEGETABLES

DAIRY

FROZEN GOODS

PANTRY ITEMS

BAKERY & DELI

NOTES:

WEEKLY MEAL
planner

	BREAKFAST	LUNCH	DINNER
Monday			
Tuesday			
Wednesday			
Thursday			
Friday			
Saturday			
Sunday			

WEEK _____

GROCERY *list*

MEAT & SEAFOOD	FRUIT & VEGETABLES	DAIRY

FROZEN GOODS	PANTRY ITEMS	BAKERY & DELI

NOTES:

WEEKLY MEAL
planner

	BREAKFAST	LUNCH	DINNER
Monday			
Tuesday			
Wednesday			
Thursday			
Friday			
Saturday			
Sunday			

WEEK _____

GROCERY *list*

MEAT & SEAFOOD	FRUIT & VEGETABLES	DAIRY

FROZEN GOODS	PANTRY ITEMS	BAKERY & DELI

NOTES:

WEEKLY MEAL
planner

	BREAKFAST	LUNCH	DINNER
Monday			
Tuesday			
Wednesday			
Thursday			
Friday			
Saturday			
Sunday			

WEEK _____

GROCERY *list*

MEAT & SEAFOOD

FRUIT & VEGETABLES

DAIRY

FROZEN GOODS

PANTRY ITEMS

BAKERY & DELI

NOTES:

WEEKLY MEAL
planner

	BREAKFAST	LUNCH	DINNER
Monday			
Tuesday			
Wednesday			
Thursday			
Friday			
Saturday			
Sunday			

WEEK _____

GROCERY *list*

MEAT & SEAFOOD

FRUIT & VEGETABLES

DAIRY

FROZEN GOODS

PANTRY ITEMS

BAKERY & DELI

NOTES:

WEEKLY MEAL
planner

	BREAKFAST	LUNCH	DINNER
Monday			
Tuesday			
Wednesday			
Thursday			
Friday			
Saturday			
Sunday			

WEEK _____

GROCERY *list*

MEAT & SEAFOOD	FRUIT & VEGETABLES	DAIRY

FROZEN GOODS	PANTRY ITEMS	BAKERY & DELI

NOTES:

WEEKLY MEAL
planner

	BREAKFAST	LUNCH	DINNER
Monday			
Tuesday			
Wednesday			
Thursday			
Friday			
Saturday			
Sunday			

WEEK _____

GROCERY *list*

MEAT & SEAFOOD

....
....
....
....
....
....
....
....
....

FRUIT & VEGETABLES

....
....
....
....
....
....
....
....
....

DAIRY

....
....
....
....
....
....
....
....
....

FROZEN GOODS

....
....
....
....
....
....
....
....
....

PANTRY ITEMS

....
....
....
....
....
....
....
....
....

BAKERY & DELI

....
....
....
....
....
....
....
....
....

NOTES:

WEEKLY MEAL
planner

	BREAKFAST	LUNCH	DINNER
Monday			
Tuesday			
Wednesday			
Thursday			
Friday			
Saturday			
Sunday			

WEEK _____

GROCERY *list*

MEAT & SEAFOOD	FRUIT & VEGETABLES	DAIRY

FROZEN GOODS	PANTRY ITEMS	BAKERY & DELI

NOTES:

WEEKLY MEAL
planner

	BREAKFAST	LUNCH	DINNER
Monday			
Tuesday			
Wednesday			
Thursday			
Friday			
Saturday			
Sunday			

WEEK _____

GROCERY *list*

MEAT & SEAFOOD

FRUIT & VEGETABLES

DAIRY

FROZEN GOODS

PANTRY ITEMS

BAKERY & DELI

NOTES:

WEEKLY MEAL
planner

	BREAKFAST	LUNCH	DINNER
Monday			
Tuesday			
Wednesday			
Thursday			
Friday			
Saturday			
Sunday			

WEEK _____

GROCERY *list*

MEAT & SEAFOOD	FRUIT & VEGETABLES	DAIRY

FROZEN GOODS	PANTRY ITEMS	BAKERY & DELI

NOTES:

WEEKLY MEAL
planner

	BREAKFAST	LUNCH	DINNER
Monday			
Tuesday			
Wednesday			
Thursday			
Friday			
Saturday			
Sunday			

WEEK _____

GROCERY *list*

MEAT & SEAFOOD	FRUIT & VEGETABLES	DAIRY

FROZEN GOODS	PANTRY ITEMS	BAKERY & DELI

NOTES:

WEEKLY MEAL
planner

	BREAKFAST	LUNCH	DINNER
Monday			
Tuesday			
Wednesday			
Thursday			
Friday			
Saturday			
Sunday			

WEEK _____

GROCERY *list*

MEAT & SEAFOOD

FRUIT & VEGETABLES

DAIRY

FROZEN GOODS

PANTRY ITEMS

BAKERY & DELI

NOTES:

WEEKLY MEAL
planner

	BREAKFAST	LUNCH	DINNER
Monday			
Tuesday			
Wednesday			
Thursday			
Friday			
Saturday			
Sunday			

WEEK _____

GROCERY *list*

MEAT & SEAFOOD

FRUIT & VEGETABLES

DAIRY

FROZEN GOODS

PANTRY ITEMS

BAKERY & DELI

NOTES:

WEEKLY MEAL
planner

	BREAKFAST	LUNCH	DINNER
Monday			
Tuesday			
Wednesday			
Thursday			
Friday			
Saturday			
Sunday			

WEEK _____

GROCERY *list*

MEAT & SEAFOOD	FRUIT & VEGETABLES	DAIRY

FROZEN GOODS	PANTRY ITEMS	BAKERY & DELI

NOTES:

WEEKLY MEAL
planner

	BREAKFAST	LUNCH	DINNER
Monday			
Tuesday			
Wednesday			
Thursday			
Friday			
Saturday			
Sunday			

WEEK _____

GROCERY *list*

MEAT & SEAFOOD

FRUIT & VEGETABLES

DAIRY

FROZEN GOODS

PANTRY ITEMS

BAKERY & DELI

NOTES:

WEEKLY MEAL *planner*

	BREAKFAST	LUNCH	DINNER
Monday			
Tuesday			
Wednesday			
Thursday			
Friday			
Saturday			
Sunday			

WEEK _____

GROCERY *list*

MEAT & SEAFOOD	FRUIT & VEGETABLES	DAIRY

FROZEN GOODS	PANTRY ITEMS	BAKERY & DELI

NOTES:

WEEKLY MEAL
planner

	BREAKFAST	LUNCH	DINNER
Monday			
Tuesday			
Wednesday			
Thursday			
Friday			
Saturday			
Sunday			

WEEK _____

GROCERY *list*

MEAT & SEAFOOD

FRUIT & VEGETABLES

DAIRY

FROZEN GOODS

PANTRY ITEMS

BAKERY & DELI

NOTES:

WEEKLY MEAL
planner

	BREAKFAST	LUNCH	DINNER
Monday			
Tuesday			
Wednesday			
Thursday			
Friday			
Saturday			
Sunday			

WEEK _____

GROCERY *list*

MEAT & SEAFOOD	FRUIT & VEGETABLES	DAIRY

FROZEN GOODS	PANTRY ITEMS	BAKERY & DELI

NOTES:

WEEKLY MEAL
planner

	BREAKFAST	LUNCH	DINNER
Monday			
Tuesday			
Wednesday			
Thursday			
Friday			
Saturday			
Sunday			

WEEK _____

GROCERY *list*

MEAT & SEAFOOD	FRUIT & VEGETABLES	DAIRY
....	....	....
....	....	....
....	....	....
....	....	....
....	....	....
....	....	....
....	....	....
....	....	....
....	....	....
....	....	....

FROZEN GOODS	PANTRY ITEMS	BAKERY & DELI
....	....	....
....	....	....
....	....	....
....	....	....
....	....	....
....	....	....
....	....	....
....	....	....

NOTES:

WEEKLY MEAL
planner

	BREAKFAST	LUNCH	DINNER
Monday			
Tuesday			
Wednesday			
Thursday			
Friday			
Saturday			
Sunday			

WEEK _____

GROCERY *list*

MEAT & SEAFOOD	FRUIT & VEGETABLES	DAIRY

FROZEN GOODS	PANTRY ITEMS	BAKERY & DELI

NOTES:

WEEKLY MEAL
planner

	BREAKFAST	LUNCH	DINNER
Monday			
Tuesday			
Wednesday			
Thursday			
Friday			
Saturday			
Sunday			

WEEK _____

GROCERY *list*

MEAT & SEAFOOD	FRUIT & VEGETABLES	DAIRY

FROZEN GOODS	PANTRY ITEMS	BAKERY & DELI

NOTES:

WEEKLY MEAL
planner

	BREAKFAST	LUNCH	DINNER
Monday			
Tuesday			
Wednesday			
Thursday			
Friday			
Saturday			
Sunday			

WEEK _____

GROCERY *list*

MEAT & SEAFOOD	FRUIT & VEGETABLES	DAIRY

FROZEN GOODS	PANTRY ITEMS	BAKERY & DELI

NOTES:

WEEKLY MEAL
planner

	BREAKFAST	LUNCH	DINNER
Monday			
Tuesday			
Wednesday			
Thursday			
Friday			
Saturday			
Sunday			

WEEK _____

GROCERY *list*

MEAT & SEAFOOD	FRUIT & VEGETABLES	DAIRY

FROZEN GOODS	PANTRY ITEMS	BAKERY & DELI

NOTES:

WEEKLY MEAL
planner

	BREAKFAST	LUNCH	DINNER
Monday			
Tuesday			
Wednesday			
Thursday			
Friday			
Saturday			
Sunday			

WEEK _____

GROCERY *list*

MEAT & SEAFOOD

....
....
....
....
....
....
....
....
....

FRUIT & VEGETABLES

....
....
....
....
....
....
....
....
....

DAIRY

....
....
....
....
....
....
....
....
....

FROZEN GOODS

....
....
....
....
....
....
....
....
....

PANTRY ITEMS

....
....
....
....
....
....
....
....
....

BAKERY & DELI

....
....
....
....
....
....
....
....
....

NOTES:

WEEKLY MEAL
planner

	BREAKFAST	LUNCH	DINNER
Monday			
Tuesday			
Wednesday			
Thursday			
Friday			
Saturday			
Sunday			

WEEK _____

GROCERY *list*

MEAT & SEAFOOD

FRUIT & VEGETABLES

DAIRY

FROZEN GOODS

PANTRY ITEMS

BAKERY & DELI

NOTES:

WEEKLY MEAL
planner

	BREAKFAST	LUNCH	DINNER
Monday			
Tuesday			
Wednesday			
Thursday			
Friday			
Saturday			
Sunday			

WEEK _____

GROCERY *list*

MEAT & SEAFOOD	FRUIT & VEGETABLES	DAIRY

FROZEN GOODS	PANTRY ITEMS	BAKERY & DELI

NOTES:

WEEKLY MEAL
planner

	BREAKFAST	LUNCH	DINNER
Monday			
Tuesday			
Wednesday			
Thursday			
Friday			
Saturday			
Sunday			

WEEK _____

GROCERY *list*

MEAT & SEAFOOD	FRUIT & VEGETABLES	DAIRY

FROZEN GOODS	PANTRY ITEMS	BAKERY & DELI

NOTES:

Made in United States
North Haven, CT
16 September 2023

41617613R00059